GRATITUDE

JOURNAL

THIS JOURNAL BELONGS TO

____

Gratitude Journal

Today I'm Thankful For

The Best Moment Of the Day Was

Thoughts And Things To Remember

My Happines Scale

Gratitude Journal

Today I'm Thankful For

The Best Moment Of the Day Was

Thoughts And Things To Remember

My Happines Scale

Gratitude Journal

Date

Today I'm Thankful For

The Best Moment Of the Day Was

Thoughts And Things To Remember

My Happines Scale

Gratitude Journal

Date

Today I'm Thankful For

The Best Moment Of the Day Was

Thoughts And Things To Remember

My Happines Scale 

Gratitude Journal

Today I'm Thankful For

The Best Moment Of the Day Was

Thoughts And Things To Remember

My Happines Scale

Gratitude Journal

Date

Today I'm Thankful For

The Best Moment Of the Day Was

Thoughts And Things To Remember

My Happines Scale 

Gratitude Journal

Date

Today I'm Thankful For

The Best Moment
Of the Day Was

Thoughts And Things
To Remember

My Happines Scale 

Gratitude Journal

Date

Today I'm Thankful For

The Best Moment Of the Day Was

Thoughts And Things To Remember

My Happines Scale

Gratitude Journal

Today I'm Thankful For

The Best Moment Of the Day Was

Thoughts And Things To Remember

My Happines Scale

Gratitude Journal

Today I'm Thankful For

The Best Moment Of the Day Was

Thoughts And Things To Remember

My Happines Scale

Gratitude Journal

Date

Today I'm Thankful For

The Best Moment Of the Day Was

Thoughts And Things To Remember

My Happines Scale

Gratitude Journal

Today I'm Thankful For

The Best Moment Of the Day Was

Thoughts And Things To Remember

My Happines Scale

Gratitude Journal

Date

Today I'm Thankful For

The Best Moment Of the Day Was

Thoughts And Things To Remember

My Happines Scale 

Gratitude Journal

Date

Today I'm Thankful For

The Best Moment Of the Day Was

Thoughts And Things To Remember

My Happines Scale 

Gratitude Journal

Date

Today I'm Thankful For

The Best Moment
Of the Day Was

Thoughts And Things
To Remember

My Happines Scale 

Gratitude Journal

Date

Today I'm Thankful For

The Best Moment Of the Day Was

Thoughts And Things To Remember

My Happines Scale 

Gratitude Journal

Date

Today I'm Thankful For

The Best Moment Of the Day Was

Thoughts And Things To Remember

My Happines Scale

Gratitude Journal

Date

Today I'm Thankful For

The Best Moment Of the Day Was

Thoughts And Things To Remember

My Happines Scale 

Gratitude Journal

Date

Today I'm Thankful For

The Best Moment Of the Day Was

Thoughts And Things To Remember

My Happines Scale 

Gratitude Journal

Date

Today I'm Thankful For

···

···

···

···

···

The Best Moment Of the Day Was

··

··

··

··

··

··

··

Thoughts And Things To Remember

··

··

··

··

··

··

··

My Happines Scale

Gratitude Journal

Today I'm Thankful For

The Best Moment Of the Day Was

Thoughts And Things To Remember

My Happines Scale

Gratitude Journal

Date

Today I'm Thankful For

The Best Moment Of the Day Was

Thoughts And Things To Remember

My Happines Scale 

Gratitude Journal

Date

Today I'm Thankful For

···
···
···
···
···
···

The Best Moment Of the Day Was

·····································
·····································
·····································
·····································
·····································
·····································
·····································

Thoughts And Things To Remember

·····································
·····································
·····································
·····································
·····································
·····································
·····································

My Happines Scale 

Gratitude Journal

Date

Today I'm Thankful For

The Best Moment Of the Day Was

Thoughts And Things To Remember

My Happines Scale

Gratitude Journal

Today I'm Thankful For

The Best Moment Of the Day Was

Thoughts And Things To Remember

My Happines Scale

Gratitude Journal

Today I'm Thankful For

The Best Moment Of the Day Was

Thoughts And Things To Remember

My Happines Scale 

Gratitude Journal

Today I'm Thankful For

The Best Moment Of the Day Was

Thoughts And Things To Remember

My Happines Scale

Gratitude Journal

Date

Today I'm Thankful For

The Best Moment Of the Day Was

Thoughts And Things To Remember

My Happines Scale

Gratitude Journal

Today I'm Thankful For

....
....
....
....
....
....

The Best Moment Of the Day Was

....
....
....
....
....
....
....

Thoughts And Things To Remember

....
....
....
....
....
....
....

My Happines Scale

Gratitude Journal

Date

Today I'm Thankful For

The Best Moment Of the Day Was

Thoughts And Things To Remember

My Happines Scale

Gratitude Journal

Today I'm Thankful For

....
....
....
....
....
....

The Best Moment Of the Day Was

....
....
....
....
....
....
....

Thoughts And Things To Remember

....
....
....
....
....
....
....

My Happines Scale

Gratitude Journal

Today I'm Thankful For

The Best Moment Of the Day Was

Thoughts And Things To Remember

My Happines Scale

Gratitude Journal

Date

Today I'm Thankful For

The Best Moment Of the Day Was

Thoughts And Things To Remember

My Happines Scale

Gratitude Journal

Today I'm Thankful For

The Best Moment Of the Day Was

Thoughts And Things To Remember

My Happines Scale 

Gratitude Journal

Today I'm Thankful For

The Best Moment Of the Day Was

Thoughts And Things To Remember

My Happines Scale

Gratitude Journal

Today I'm Thankful For

The Best Moment Of the Day Was

Thoughts And Things To Remember

My Happines Scale

Gratitude Journal

Date

Today I'm Thankful For

The Best Moment Of the Day Was

Thoughts And Things To Remember

My Happines Scale 

Gratitude Journal

Date

Today I'm Thankful For

The Best Moment Of the Day Was

Thoughts And Things To Remember

My Happines Scale

Gratitude Journal

Date

Today I'm Thankful For

....
....
....
....
....

The Best Moment Of the Day Was

....
....
....
....
....

Thoughts And Things To Remember

....
....
....
....
....

My Happines Scale

Gratitude Journal

Date

Today I'm Thankful For

The Best Moment Of the Day Was

Thoughts And Things To Remember

My Happines Scale

Gratitude Journal

Date

Today I'm Thankful For

The Best Moment Of the Day Was

Thoughts And Things To Remember

My Happines Scale 

Gratitude Journal

Date

Today I'm Thankful For

The Best Moment Of the Day Was

Thoughts And Things To Remember

My Happines Scale 

Gratitude Journal

Today I'm Thankful For

The Best Moment Of the Day Was

Thoughts And Things To Remember

My Happines Scale

Gratitude Journal

Date

Today I'm Thankful For

The Best Moment Of the Day Was

Thoughts And Things To Remember

My Happines Scale

Gratitude Journal

Today I'm Thankful For

The Best Moment Of the Day Was

Thoughts And Things To Remember

My Happines Scale

Gratitude Journal

Date

Today I'm Thankful For

The Best Moment Of the Day Was

Thoughts And Things To Remember

My Happines Scale

Gratitude Journal

Date

Today I'm Thankful For

The Best Moment Of the Day Was

Thoughts And Things To Remember

My Happines Scale

Gratitude Journal

Today I'm Thankful For

The Best Moment
Of the Day Was

Thoughts And Things
To Remember

My Happines Scale 

Gratitude Journal

Date

Today I'm Thankful For

The Best Moment Of the Day Was

Thoughts And Things To Remember

My Happines Scale

Gratitude Journal

Date

Today I'm Thankful For

....

....

....

....

....

....

The Best Moment Of the Day Was

....

....

....

....

....

....

....

Thoughts And Things To Remember

....

....

....

....

....

....

....

My Happines Scale 

Gratitude Journal

Today I'm Thankful For

The Best Moment Of the Day Was

Thoughts And Things To Remember

My Happines Scale

Gratitude Journal

Today I'm Thankful For

The Best Moment Of the Day Was

Thoughts And Things To Remember

My Happines Scale

Gratitude Journal

Today I'm Thankful For

The Best Moment Of the Day Was

Thoughts And Things To Remember

My Happines Scale

Gratitude Journal

Date

Today I'm Thankful For

The Best Moment Of the Day Was

Thoughts And Things To Remember

My Happines Scale 

Gratitude Journal

Today I'm Thankful For

The Best Moment Of the Day Was

Thoughts And Things To Remember

My Happines Scale

Gratitude Journal

Date

Today I'm Thankful For

The Best Moment Of the Day Was

Thoughts And Things To Remember

My Happines Scale 

Gratitude Journal

Date

Today I'm Thankful For

The Best Moment Of the Day Was

Thoughts And Things To Remember

My Happines Scale

Gratitude Journal

Date

Today I'm Thankful For

The Best Moment Of the Day Was

Thoughts And Things To Remember

My Happines Scale 

Gratitude Journal

Today I'm Thankful For

The Best Moment Of the Day Was

Thoughts And Things To Remember

My Happines Scale

Gratitude Journal

Date

Today I'm Thankful For

....

....

....

....

....

The Best Moment Of the Day Was

....

....

....

....

....

....

....

Thoughts And Things To Remember

....

....

....

....

....

....

....

My Happines Scale 

Gratitude Journal

Date

Today I'm Thankful For

The Best Moment
Of the Day Was

Thoughts And Things
To Remember

My Happines Scale 

Gratitude Journal

Date

Today I'm Thankful For

The Best Moment
Of the Day Was

Thoughts And Things
To Remember

My Happines Scale 

Gratitude Journal

Today I'm Thankful For

The Best Moment Of the Day Was

Thoughts And Things To Remember

My Happines Scale

Gratitude Journal

Today I'm Thankful For

The Best Moment Of the Day Was

Thoughts And Things To Remember

My Happines Scale 

Gratitude Journal

Date

Today I'm Thankful For

The Best Moment Of the Day Was

Thoughts And Things To Remember

My Happines Scale

Gratitude Journal

Date

Today I'm Thankful For

The Best Moment Of the Day Was

Thoughts And Things To Remember

My Happines Scale

Gratitude Journal

Date

Today I'm Thankful For

The Best Moment Of the Day Was

Thoughts And Things To Remember

My Happines Scale

Gratitude Journal

Date

Today I'm Thankful For

The Best Moment Of the Day Was

Thoughts And Things To Remember

My Happines Scale 

Gratitude Journal

Date

Today I'm Thankful For

The Best Moment Of the Day Was

Thoughts And Things To Remember

My Happines Scale ☆☆☆☆☆

Gratitude Journal

Today I'm Thankful For

The Best Moment Of the Day Was

Thoughts And Things To Remember

My Happines Scale

Gratitude Journal

Date

Today I'm Thankful For

The Best Moment
Of the Day Was

Thoughts And Things
To Remember

My Happines Scale

Gratitude Journal

Date

Today I'm Thankful For

The Best Moment
Of the Day Was

Thoughts And Things
To Remember

My Happines Scale 

Gratitude Journal

Date

Today I'm Thankful For

....

....

....

....

....

The Best Moment Of the Day Was

....

....

....

....

....

Thoughts And Things To Remember

....

....

....

....

....

My Happines Scale

Gratitude Journal

Date

Today I'm Thankful For

The Best Moment Of the Day Was

Thoughts And Things To Remember

My Happines Scale 

Gratitude Journal

Today I'm Thankful For

The Best Moment Of the Day Was

Thoughts And Things To Remember

My Happines Scale

Gratitude Journal

Date

Today I'm Thankful For

The Best Moment Of the Day Was

Thoughts And Things To Remember

My Happines Scale 

Gratitude Journal

Today I'm Thankful For

The Best Moment Of the Day Was

Thoughts And Things To Remember

My Happines Scale

Gratitude Journal

Date

Today I'm Thankful For

The Best Moment Of the Day Was

Thoughts And Things To Remember

My Happines Scale 

Gratitude Journal

Date

Today I'm Thankful For

The Best Moment Of the Day Was

Thoughts And Things To Remember

My Happines Scale

Gratitude Journal

Date

Today I'm Thankful For

The Best Moment Of the Day Was

Thoughts And Things To Remember

My Happines Scale 

Gratitude Journal

Today I'm Thankful For

The Best Moment Of the Day Was

Thoughts And Things To Remember

My Happines Scale

Gratitude Journal

Date

Today I'm Thankful For

The Best Moment Of the Day Was

Thoughts And Things To Remember

My Happines Scale 

Gratitude Journal

Date

Today I'm Thankful For

The Best Moment Of the Day Was

Thoughts And Things To Remember

My Happines Scale

Gratitude Journal

Date

Today I'm Thankful For

The Best Moment Of the Day Was

Thoughts And Things To Remember

My Happines Scale

Gratitude Journal

Today I'm Thankful For

The Best Moment Of the Day Was

Thoughts And Things To Remember

My Happines Scale

Gratitude Journal

Today I'm Thankful For

The Best Moment Of the Day Was

Thoughts And Things To Remember

My Happines Scale

Gratitude Journal

Today I'm Thankful For

The Best Moment Of the Day Was

Thoughts And Things To Remember

My Happines Scale

Gratitude Journal

Today I'm Thankful For

The Best Moment Of the Day Was

Thoughts And Things To Remember

My Happines Scale 

Gratitude Journal

Date

Today I'm Thankful For

The Best Moment Of the Day Was

Thoughts And Things To Remember

My Happines Scale 

Gratitude Journal

Date

Today I'm Thankful For

The Best Moment Of the Day Was

Thoughts And Things To Remember

My Happines Scale 

Gratitude Journal

Date

Today I'm Thankful For

The Best Moment Of the Day Was

Thoughts And Things To Remember

My Happines Scale

Gratitude Journal

Date

Today I'm Thankful For

The Best Moment Of the Day Was

Thoughts And Things To Remember

My Happines Scale

Gratitude Journal

Date

Today I'm Thankful For

The Best Moment Of the Day Was

Thoughts And Things To Remember

My Happines Scale

Gratitude Journal

Date

Today I'm Thankful For

The Best Moment Of the Day Was

Thoughts And Things To Remember

My Happines Scale 

Gratitude Journal

Date

Today I'm Thankful For

The Best Moment Of the Day Was

Thoughts And Things To Remember

My Happines Scale 

Gratitude Journal

Date

Today I'm Thankful For

The Best Moment Of the Day Was

Thoughts And Things To Remember

My Happines Scale 

Gratitude Journal

Today I'm Thankful For

The Best Moment Of the Day Was

Thoughts And Things To Remember

My Happines Scale

Gratitude Journal

Date

Today I'm Thankful For

....
....
....
....
....
....

The Best Moment Of the Day Was

....
....
....
....
....
....
....

Thoughts And Things To Remember

....
....
....
....
....
....
....

My Happines Scale 

Gratitude Journal

Today I'm Thankful For

The Best Moment Of the Day Was

Thoughts And Things To Remember

My Happines Scale 

Gratitude Journal

Today I'm Thankful For

The Best Moment Of the Day Was

Thoughts And Things To Remember

My Happines Scale

Gratitude Journal

Date

Today I'm Thankful For

The Best Moment Of the Day Was

Thoughts And Things To Remember

My Happines Scale ☆☆☆☆☆

Gratitude Journal

Date

Today I'm Thankful For

The Best Moment Of the Day Was

Thoughts And Things To Remember

My Happines Scale

Gratitude Journal

Today I'm Thankful For

. . . .

. . . .

. . . .

. . . .

. . . .

The Best Moment Of the Day Was	Thoughts And Things To Remember
. . . .	. . . .
. . . .	. . . .
. . . .	. . . .
. . . .	. . . .
. . . .	. . . .

My Happines Scale

Gratitude Journal

Date

Today I'm Thankful For

The Best Moment Of the Day Was

Thoughts And Things To Remember

My Happines Scale 

Gratitude Journal

Date

Today I'm Thankful For

The Best Moment Of the Day Was

Thoughts And Things To Remember

My Happines Scale

Gratitude Journal

Date

Today I'm Thankful For

. . . .

. . . .

. . . .

. . . .

. . . .

. . . .

The Best Moment Of the Day Was

. . . .

. . . .

. . . .

. . . .

. . . .

. . . .

Thoughts And Things To Remember

. . . .

. . . .

. . . .

. . . .

. . . .

. . . .

My Happines Scale

Gratitude Journal

Date

Today I'm Thankful For

The Best Moment Of the Day Was

Thoughts And Things To Remember

My Happines Scale

Gratitude Journal

Date

Today I'm Thankful For

The Best Moment Of the Day Was

Thoughts And Things To Remember

My Happines Scale

Gratitude Journal

Today I'm Thankful For

The Best Moment Of the Day Was

Thoughts And Things To Remember

My Happines Scale

Gratitude Journal

Date

Today I'm Thankful For

The Best Moment Of the Day Was

Thoughts And Things To Remember

My Happines Scale 

Gratitude Journal

Date

Today I'm Thankful For

The Best Moment Of the Day Was

Thoughts And Things To Remember

My Happines Scale 

Gratitude Journal

Today I'm Thankful For

The Best Moment Of the Day Was

Thoughts And Things To Remember

My Happines Scale

Gratitude Journal

Date

Today I'm Thankful For

The Best Moment Of the Day Was

Thoughts And Things To Remember

My Happines Scale

Gratitude Journal

Today I'm Thankful For

The Best Moment Of the Day Was

Thoughts And Things To Remember

My Happines Scale ☆☆☆☆☆

Gratitude Journal

Date

Today I'm Thankful For

The Best Moment Of the Day Was

Thoughts And Things To Remember

My Happines Scale

Gratitude Journal

Today I'm Thankful For

The Best Moment Of the Day Was

Thoughts And Things To Remember

My Happines Scale 

Gratitude Journal

Today I'm Thankful For

The Best Moment Of the Day Was

Thoughts And Things To Remember

My Happines Scale

Gratitude Journal

Today I'm Thankful For

The Best Moment Of the Day Was

Thoughts And Things To Remember

My Happines Scale

Gratitude Journal

Date

Today I'm Thankful For

The Best Moment Of the Day Was

Thoughts And Things To Remember

My Happines Scale ☆ ☆ ☆ ☆ ☆